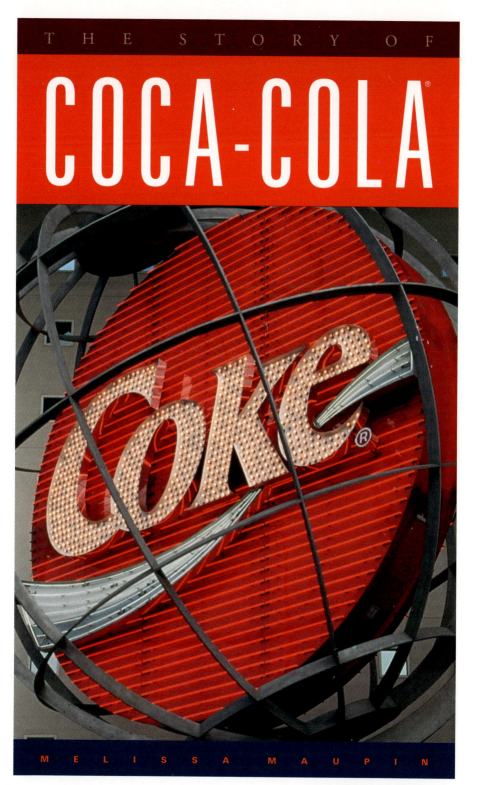

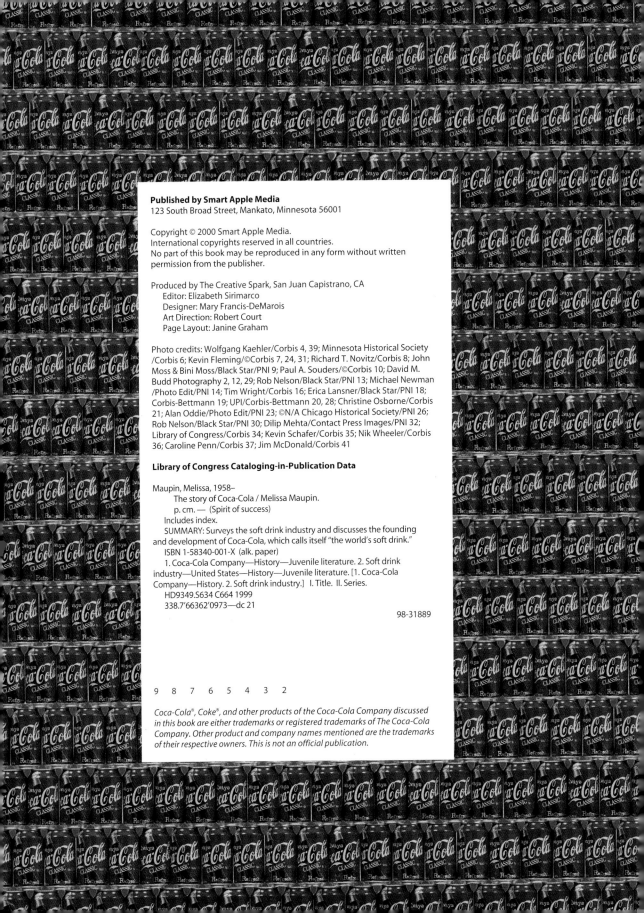

Published by Smart Apple Media
123 South Broad Street, Mankato, Minnesota 56001

Copyright © 2000 Smart Apple Media.
International copyrights reserved in all countries.
No part of this book may be reproduced in any form without written permission from the publisher.

Produced by The Creative Spark, San Juan Capistrano, CA
    Editor: Elizabeth Sirimarco
    Designer: Mary Francis-DeMarois
    Art Direction: Robert Court
    Page Layout: Janine Graham

Photo credits: Wolfgang Kaehler/Corbis 4, 39; Minnesota Historical Society/Corbis 6; Kevin Fleming/©Corbis 7, 24, 31; Richard T. Novitz/Corbis 8; John Moss & Bini Moss/Black Star/PNI 9; Paul A. Souders/©Corbis 10; David M. Budd Photography 2, 12, 29; Rob Nelson/Black Star/PNI 13; Michael Newman/Photo Edit/PNI 14; Tim Wright/Corbis 16; Erica Lansner/Black Star/PNI 18; Corbis-Bettmann 19; UPI/Corbis-Bettmann 20, 28; Christine Osborne/Corbis 21; Alan Oddie/Photo Edit/PNI 23; ©N/A Chicago Historical Society/PNI 26; Rob Nelson/Black Star/PNI 30; Dilip Mehta/Contact Press Images/PNI 32; Library of Congress/Corbis 34; Kevin Schafer/Corbis 35; Nik Wheeler/Corbis 36; Caroline Penn/Corbis 37; Jim McDonald/Corbis 41

Library of Congress Cataloging-in-Publication Data

Maupin, Melissa, 1958–
    The story of Coca-Cola / Melissa Maupin.
      p. cm. — (Spirit of success)
    Includes index.
    SUMMARY: Surveys the soft drink industry and discusses the founding and development of Coca-Cola, which calls itself "the world's soft drink."
    ISBN 1-58340-001-X (alk. paper)
    1. Coca-Cola Company—History—Juvenile literature. 2. Soft drink industry—United States—History—Juvenile literature. [1. Coca-Cola Company—History. 2. Soft drink industry.] I. Title. II. Series.
    HD9349.S634 C664 1999
    338.7'66362'0973—dc 21
                                                   98-31889

9 8 7 6 5 4 3 2

Coca-Cola®, Coke®, and other products of the Coca-Cola Company discussed in this book are either trademarks or registered trademarks of The Coca-Cola Company. Other product and company names mentioned are the trademarks of their respective owners. This is not an official publication.

Table of Contents

The Birth of Coca-Cola   4

Taking Coca-Cola Home   10

New Looks, New Ideas   16

Marketing Coca-Cola   24

The World's Favorite Soft Drink   32

Important Moments   42

Glossary   44

Index   46

Further Information   48

The Birth of Coca-Cola

Coca-Cola® calls itself "the world's soft drink," and for a good reason. People in nearly 200 countries drink one billion, 8-ounce servings of Coca-Cola products every day. So much Coke® has been produced since the first batch in 1886, that if you put it all into 8-ounce bottles and stacked them up, the bottles would tower 325 miles (520 kilometers) into the sky—60 times taller than Mount Everest, the tallest mountain in the world! Coca-Cola didn't become the number one soft drink overnight, of course. It started more than 100 years ago with a man named John Pemberton.

Today Coke is a **carbonated** soft drink, but it actually started out with no bubbles at all. Dr. John Pemberton, a **pharmacist** from Atlanta, Georgia, developed the formula for Coca-Cola syrup in a three-legged brass pot. The two chief ingredients were the **extracts** of the kola nut and the coca plant. Pemberton spent a lot of time making **tonics** for illnesses and health problems. He may have been working on a headache cure the day he created the syrup that would soon become Coca-Cola.

Pemberton liked the way his new tonic tasted, and he decided to take it to Jacob's Pharmacy, the largest pharmacy in Atlanta. Drugstores at the time had soda fountains where customers could sit and enjoy drinks and other refreshments. Pemberton asked the manager, Willis Venable, to mix his tonic with water and sell it at the soda fountain as a tonic for headaches and tiredness. Venable liked the drink as well and agreed to sell it for five cents a glass.

Pemberton's partner and bookkeeper, Frank Robinson, was the one who actually suggested the name "Coca-Cola" for the drink because he thought the two capital "C's" would look good in advertisements. He also drew the letters of the name in the same graceful style of print used today. A few weeks after Jacob's Pharmacy began selling Coca-Cola, Pemberton and Robinson ran the first advertisement for the product in the *Atlanta Daily*

carbonated

Relating to the use of carbon dioxide to make a soft drink bubbly.

pharmacist

A person who prepares and distributes medicines.

extracts

A concentrated substance that is extracted, or taken out of, its source, such as a plant or fruit. An extract has a stronger flavor or smell than its source.

tonics

Mixtures designed to refresh and restore.

slogan

A short, attention-getting phrase used in advertising.

In the 19th century, pharmacists such as John Pemberton mixed together different ingredients to make medicine instead of buying medications from drug companies. Sometimes they invented new medicines for headaches or colds to help their customers feel better.

Journal. The ad claimed Coca-Cola was "Delicious! Refreshing! Exhilarating! Invigorating!" "Delicious and Refreshing" became the first official **slogan** used by Coca-Cola.

No one is sure how it happened, but later that same year, someone accidentally added carbonated water to the Coke syrup instead of plain water. Customers who tried the new bubbly drink liked it better, and it has been served as a carbonated drink since that time.

Customers liked Coca-Cola, but it was not an instant success. Pemberton sold only 25 gallons of syrup the first year and received about $50 for his trouble. He still believed in his tonic, but his health was beginning to fail, and he didn't feel he had the strength or money to promote Coca-Cola properly.

In 1891, a man named Asa Candler bought Coca-Cola from Pemberton for $2,300. One reason Candler was interested in this product was that he had suffered from severe headaches all his life. He had heard that the Coca-Cola tonic could help, and when he tried it, he found that it did, in fact, ease his headaches. After buying the Coca-Cola Company, Candler even advertised the drink as "The Wonderful Nerve and Brain Tonic."

Candler was a hard worker who believed that advertising would boost the sales of his new soft drink.

Soda fountains were a popular place for friends to get together at the end of the 19th century. Coca-Cola became a favorite refreshment once Asa Candler began to advertise the soft drink.

Asa Candler, who bought Coca-Cola in 1891, gave away a variety of gifts that featured the Coca-Cola logo. Some popular items included clocks, calendars, puzzles, playing cards, and posters. Today people around the world collect these old-fashioned promotional items.

A woman from Kenya, an African nation, enjoys a Coke. The Coca-Cola Company is the number one beverage company in the world. In 1994, soft-drink fans enjoyed more than 773 million servings of Coca-Cola products. 1998 estimates suggest that number has increased to an amazing one billion servings daily.

> **trademark**
>
> *A symbol or name that belongs legally and exclusively to one company. It may also refer to something that is unique about a company.*

He sent coupons for free drinks to pharmacies that sold his syrup and put the Coca-Cola name on calendars, coasters, posters, clocks, and other items. Within four years, soda fountains in every state and territory of the United States sold Coke syrup.

Candler registered the name "Coca-Cola" with the U.S. Patent Office as an official **trademark** in 1893. He wanted customers to call the drink by the original name, "Coca-Cola," even though people were already calling the product by a new nickname, Coke. Eventually, in 1945, the Coca-Cola Company also registered the name "Coke" as a trademark.

Taking Coca-Cola Home

In the beginning, Coca-Cola® was sold only as a syrup, which had to be mixed with water at soda fountains. Mr. Candler had no interest in putting the drink in bottles at the time because it was a slow and awkward task. The bottles were sealed with a cork and wire hook, and when opened, the cork went down into the bottle and stayed there. This made cleaning and refilling bottles difficult and time-consuming. The bottles also tended to explode, which could be dangerous and costly.

Even with these problems, one soda fountain owner, Joseph Biedenharn, thought bottling the popular drink made sense. He wanted to sell Coke® to people who lived outside of the city and were unable to visit soda fountains very often. In 1894, he set up a bottling machine in his store and became the first person to bottle Coke. Now people could enjoy Coca-Cola at home, on a picnic, or almost anywhere they wanted.

In 1899, two businessmen from Tennessee, Benjamin Thomas and Joseph Whitehead, paid Candler just $1 for the right to bottle and sell Coca-Cola throughout the United States. Since setting up bottling plants was expensive, they came up with the idea of **independent bottlers.** They signed **contracts** with businesspeople in various states who wanted to bottle Coke. The independent bottlers provided the employees, factories, bottles, and machinery. The Coca-Cola Company provided the Coca-Cola syrup and helped the bottlers with training, advertising, and the running of their businesses. Using this bottling method, Coca-Cola could sell its soft drink across the country—and eventually around the world.

There were many other soda fountain drinks during the late 1880s and early 1900s when Coke was getting its start. Most of these drinks had fruity flavors, such as orange, lemon, and strawberry. Once bottles of Coca-Cola became popular across the country, other soft-drink companies naturally wanted to make similar beverages.

independent bottlers

Businesspeople who pay to set up a bottling plant with their money but are given assistance from the soft-drink company. The Coca-Cola Company supplies its independent bottlers with syrup to produce its products.

contracts

Written agreements made between two parties promising to meet certain obligations.

Some even copied the style of lettering Coca-Cola used. Even Dr. Pemberton, the man who made the original batch of Coca-Cola, began creating new tonics and selling them. He called one of his drinks "Yum Yum." One Coke bottler estimated that there were more than 150 brands trying to copy Coke. Among the competitors were King Cola, Cola Ree, Gay-Ola, Cold Cola, and Candy Cola.

Coca-Cola did not want to lose its customers to imitators, and company officials decided to find a way to make Coca-Cola stand out. At that time, all soft-drink bottlers used bottles with straight sides. Coke bottlers

Asa Candler wasn't interested in bottling his soft drink, but today factories all over the world have teamed up with the Coca-Cola Company to bottle the popular soda.

According to the Coca-Cola Company, the shape of the Coke bottle was designed so that "a person could recognize it in the dark, so shaped that, even if broken, a person could tell at a glance what it was."

Restaurants and diners still serve Coca-Cola in the company's popular bell-shaped glasses, designed in 1929.

decided to try something new. In 1915, they hired the Root Glass Company to design the unique, curved-glass Coca-Cola bottle.

There are two stories about how the glass company got the idea for the design. One legend says that the shape was similar to a hobble skirt—a long, tight skirt popular with women at the time. The other explanation is that the company was trying to mimic the shape of a coca bean, one of the ingredients in Coca-Cola. Either way, the curved bottle was different enough from other bottles that Coca-Cola was able to register it as a trademark. In 1929, after the hobble-skirt bottle proved successful, Coke designed a special bell-shaped fountain glass for serving the soft drink. These familiar glasses are still sold and used today.

New Looks, New Ideas

Mr. Candler made a nice profit when he finally decided to sell the Coca-Cola® Company. In 1919, a banker named Ernest Woodruff bought the business for $25 million. Four years later, Mr. Woodruff's son, Robert Winship Woodruff, took over the company's leadership when he was elected president. The younger Woodruff stayed actively involved in the company for the next 60 years.

Robert Woodruff believed in quality and even started a training program for soda fountain operators to make sure they served the drink correctly. He took advantage of new **technology** to help boost sales of Coca-Cola. In the early 1920s, for example, Coke was sold from the first soft-drink vending machines—simple, refrigerated ice chests with tops that opened. The ice chests allowed workers to buy Coca-Cola in offices, factories, and businesses. In 1933, visitors to the Chicago World's Fair were surprised by another new invention—the automatic fountain dispenser. Instead of mixing carbonated water with syrup, Coke® was now premixed and served cold from a single dispenser.

Although Americans loved Coke, it was only sold in five other countries outside of the United States when Mr. Woodruff bought the business. Woodruff was certain he could sell Coke in other countries as well, and he set out to do just that. In 1928, the Coca-Cola Company discovered a clever way to reach people from nearly every country in the world. Coca-Cola became the first soft drink served at the Olympic Games. The company shipped 1,000 cases of Coke to the 1928 Summer Olympics in Amsterdam. Vendors wearing clothes with the Coca-Cola name sold cold drinks to about 40,000 spectators in the stadium. Others sold Coke outside the stadium at small stands called "winkles."

By the time the United States entered World War II in the 1940s, Coca-Cola was bottled in 44 countries—including nations at war against the United States. During the war,

technology
Science that is used to improve everyday life.

Woodruff's goal was to provide every man and woman in uniform with Coke—no matter where they were in the world. Coca-Cola ended up opening 64 plants overseas during the war. Not only did this familiar drink from home lift the spirits of American troops, it also gave the residents of other countries a chance to try Coca-Cola for the first time.

While the taste of Coca-Cola stayed the same throughout the years, the containers in which it came changed with the times. For 50 years, Coke was sold at soda fountains in

Automatic fountain dispensers were first introduced in 1933 to mix soft-drink syrup and carbonated water quickly and neatly.

the bell-shaped glasses or in the traditional curved bottles. In the 1950s, Coke introduced a choice of bottles in 10, 12, and 26-ounce sizes. These larger-sized bottles were an instant hit. Metal cans hit the scene in the 1960s and quickly became the most convenient and popular packaging for soft drinks. In 1978, Coca-Cola made history when it introduced the first plastic PET (polyethylene terphthalate) bottle, which is now used by most soft-drink bottlers. In the 1980s and 1990s, **consumers** grew more concerned about

consumers

People who buy and consume, or use, a product or service.

Two soldiers treat their dates to refreshments at a soda fountain during World War I.

Soldiers in Italy during World War II enjoy the first Cokes to reach U.S. soldiers in Europe.

pollution and the environment. Coke responded by encouraging consumers to **recycle** aluminum cans. It also developed bottles that could be recycled.

In 1960, Coca-Cola added its first new product line, Fanta®. Fanta products, which came in a variety of fruit flavors such as orange and grape, had been sold by Coke bottlers in other countries for many years. It was a very popular drink and still ranks as one of the top five soft drinks around the world.

In 1996, Americans recycled nearly 64 percent of the 99 billion aluminum soft-drink cans produced. They also recycled 38.6 percent of PET plastic bottles and 36 percent of glass bottles.

recycle

To process a used material (such as plastic, aluminum, or glass) so that it can be used again.

stimulants

Compounds, such as caffeine, that can make a person feel more awake or energetic. If people ingest too much of a stimulant, they can feel nervous or jittery.

Coke added Sprite® to its lineup a year after Fanta. The name "Sprite" came from an earlier advertisement for Coca-Cola. In the 1940s, Coke had used a little elf-like man with a big smile in its ads. He had white hair and wore a bottle cap for a hat. Eventually he became known as the "Sprite Boy," since "sprite" means an elfish creature. When Coca-Cola developed its citrus-flavored drink, company leaders thought the short, spunky name of Sprite fit the product well. Unfortunately, another drink company was using the name. Coke had to buy the right to use the Sprite name and register it legally.

Tab®, Coke's first low-calorie drink, was introduced in 1963. In 1982, the company introduced Diet Coke®, or Light Coke®, as it is known in some countries. Diet Coke quickly became the most popular low-calorie drink in the world. While Diet Coke sales are much higher than sales of Tab, Coca-Cola Company still produces a small quantity of Tab to satisfy its small, but loyal, following. Coke purchased the Minute Maid Company, producer of juice products, in 1960 and introduced a new line of Minute Maid® soft drinks to the United States in 1987. One of Coke's most recent additions is Surge®, introduced in 1997 as a "fully loaded citrus soda," implying that it is jam-packed with two **stimulants,** caffeine and sugar.

Coca-Cola Products

1886	Coca-Cola	**1983**	Caffeine-free products
1960	Fanta flavors	**1985**	Cherry Coke, New Coke
1961	Sprite	**1987**	Minute Maid Orange Drink
1963	Tab	**1990**	Powerade
1966	Fresca	**1994**	Fruitopia
1972	Mr. Pib	**1997**	Surge
1979	Mello Yello		
1982	Diet Coke		

All products are registered trademarks of The Coca-Cola Company.

Marketing Coca-Cola

One reason Coca-Cola® has become so successful is the clever way the company markets its soft drinks. To **market** a product means to come up with a plan that will convince consumers to buy it. Coca-Cola took Mr. Candler's early interest in advertising and continued to look for interesting ways to spread the word about its products. After Coca-Cola was bottled and sold nationwide, the Coca-Cola Company used famous artists such as Norman Rockwell to paint heart-warming images of families enjoying Coca-Cola. It used the artwork in ads for magazines and newspapers.

The company also continued to add catchy new slogans to its early one, "Delicious and Refreshing." As radio and television became increasingly commonplace in homes worldwide, the company expanded these slogans into jingles, songs written for an advertising campaign. The jingles were recorded by well-known singing groups of the time, such as the Supremes and Jan and Dean in the 1960s. One of the company's most popular slogans was "Things Go Better With Coke" from the 1960s, which was recorded by more than 60 different singers and musical groups. "The Real Thing," first used in 1942, was reintroduced in the late 1960s. "Coke Is It!" was the choice for the 1980s.

Pairing up products with celebrities is a common way to advertise today, but Coca-Cola combined famous faces with its products as early as 1950. Coke sponsored its first television program, *The Edgar Bergan and Charlie McCarthy Show*, that year. Edgar Bergan was an actor and ventriloquist, and Charlie was his sidekick dummy.

Since then, Coke has used many movie actors, singers, and sports figures to promote its drinks. In the 1970s, Coke used its slogan "Have a Coke and a Smile" as the theme for one of the best-loved television commercials of the decade. The commercial featured a young boy who shared a cold Coke with Pittsburgh Steelers tackle "Mean" Joe Green after a professional football game. In the end, Mr. Green tossed the boy his jersey as a souvenir and also gave him a smile.

market
To promote or advertise a product to consumers.

ad campaigns

Planned series of ads with a common theme.

In the mid-1980s, Coca-Cola still produced the top selling soft drink, but Pepsi® was becoming more and more popular. Pepsi ran two successful **ad campaigns.** The "Pepsi Generation" ads claimed that Pepsi was the drink for young, hip consumers. The ads worked. Pepsi sales climbed, and the so-called "cola wars" began.

The second Pepsi campaign, "The Pepsi Challenge," hit Coke even harder. Pepsi began airing television commercials with ordinary people taking The Pepsi Challenge by

"Delicious and Refreshing," Coca-Cola's first advertising slogan, appeared in advertisements and on signs for many years.

Coca-Cola had been the favorite soft drink of America's youth for a century when Pepsi began an ad campaign in the 1980s to attract young people.

executives

A company's leaders, such as its president and top managers. Executives make important decisions for a company.

tasting Pepsi and Coca-Cola side-by-side without knowing which was which. Many tasters who said they were Coke drinkers chose Pepsi over Coke. This made Coca-Cola nervous.

After studying the problem, the Coca-Cola Company decided that people's tastes must be changing. Company **executives** believed people wanted a soft drink that tasted more like Pepsi, which was lighter and sweeter than Coke. The Coca-Cola Company did something no one thought it would ever do: It announced the plan to get rid of the

President Dwight Eisenhower has a Coke—and a smile—1952.

The so-called cola wars caused Coca-Cola to change its formula to attract customers, but the plan backfired.

100-year-old Coke formula and introduce a sweeter, softer Coke. Everyone, including Pepsi, was surprised. Many loyal Coke drinkers were angry and refused to drink New Coke®. During this period, Pepsi sales increased, and it briefly became the number one soft drink.

After letters and phone calls poured in asking for the old Coke, the Coca-Cola Company announced the return of the original formula with a new name—Coca-Cola Classic®. Some Coke drinkers believe the Coke Company didn't return to the exact formula it used before, but no

Brian Dyson was the president of the Coca-Cola Company in 1985, the year it introduced New Coke, a lighter, sweeter cola. The public complained, and soon Coca-Cola Classic, with the same taste people had enjoyed for a century, made its comeback.

one really knows for sure, since the formula has been a well-kept secret from the beginning. Dropping the traditional Coke formula was clearly a mistake, but the company learned something: It discovered how loyal Coke drinkers were.

Popular Coke Slogans

Delicious and Refreshing *(1886)*

The Great National Temperance *(1906)*

Three Million a Day *(1917)*

Around the Corner from Everywhere *(1927)*

The Pause that Refreshes *(1929)*

The Only Thing Like Coca-Cola Is Coca-Cola Itself. It's the Real Thing *(1942)*

What You Want Is a Coke *(1952)*

Things Go Better with Coke *(1963)*

It's the Real Thing *(1970)*

I'd Like to Buy the World a Coke *(1971)*

Have a Coke and a Smile *(1979)*

Coke Is It! *(1982)*

Can't Beat the Feeling *(1989)*

Can't Beat the Real Thing *(1990)*

Always Coca-Cola *(1993)*

The World's Favorite Soft Drink

Many Coke® fans enjoy collecting Coca-Cola® items, just like other people collect baseball cards, coins, or stamps. Any object that bears the names of Coca-Cola products is considered a collectible. Some early Coke items may be worth a good deal of money, but not all collectibles are antiques.

People can find all types of Coke collectibles, from ceiling fans and ballpoint pens to toys and T-shirts. The Coca-Cola Company doesn't actually make all these things. Manufacturers pay Coke a fee for a **license** to use the Coca-Cola names.

One collectible that continues to delight Coke fans of all ages is the white polar bear Coke used in its early-1990s television commercials with the slogan, "Always Coca-Cola." The bear is still sold as a stuffed animal and makes appearances on other items, particularly in the winter.

Christmas ornaments and holiday items have long been favorite Coke collectibles. The first were made in 1931 when an artist named Haddon Sundblom was hired to paint Santa Claus for Coca-Cola ads. Before his drawings, there were many versions of what Santa Claus looked like—some artists drew him as an elf, others pictured him as tall and thin. Sundblom's vision of Santa as the chubby, cheery man with a great white beard and red, round cheeks is how Americans still think of Santa today.

In 1990, Coca-Cola opened a three-story pavilion in Atlanta, Georgia, called the World of Coca-Cola. Since then, it has opened two more, one in Las Vegas and another in New York City. These museums celebrate the history of Coca-Cola and its products with a series of exhibits displaying more than 1,000 pieces of Coke **memorabilia.**

Visitors can learn about the history of the company and the soft-drink bottling industry or view 10-minute

license
Permission granted to use a company name, slogan, or image.

memorabilia
Objects that are reminders of the past.

Artist Haddon Sundblom's Santa, which he first drew for a Coke ad, caught on with the public. Coke still makes holiday paper, napkins, ornaments and even special holiday bottles featuring this jolly image of Santa Claus.

The World of Coke museum in Atlanta features three stories of Coca-Cola memorabilia. Most visitors say their favorite part of the attraction is the tasting room, where they can sample many different Coke products from around the world.

films that highlight famous Coke television commercials from the past. On display are old soda fountains and early bottling machines. The best part comes as visitors exit the museum, and everyone gets to try samples of all the Coca-Cola products, including exotic ones that Coke bottlers sell in other countries, such as Maaza®, a noncarbonated mango-flavored drink from India, and Lift®, a lemon-lime beverage from Australia.

Coca-Cola has come a long way since Mr. Pemberton's discovery more than 100 years ago. The Coca-Cola Company

Visitors to the World of Coke enjoy Coca-Cola products as they view popular commercials from the past.

is the largest beverage company in the world, with 195 countries bottling and distributing the drink around the globe. Pemberton and Candler would be delighted to learn that Coca-Cola is also still the most popular fountain drink around.

According to the Coca-Cola Company, it took 22 years to sell its first one billion servings of Coke products. At present, it serves one billion servings of its soft drinks in a

An Egyptian advertisement for Coca-Cola.

Annual International Consumption of Coca-Cola Products*

Country	8 oz. servings per person	Country	8 oz. servings per person
India	3	Japan	150
China	6	Hungary	153
Indonesia	10	South Africa	155
Russia	21	Benelux/Denmark	196
Egypt	28	Canada	196
Romania	57	Spain	201
Morocco	61	Germany	203
Thailand	69	Argentina	207
Zimbabwe	69	Venezuela	219
Korea	71	Israel	267
France	88	Norway	272
Italy	95	Australia	276
Columbia	116	Chile	325
Great Britain	118	Mexico	371
Philippines	130	United States	376
Brazil	134		

Source: The Coca-Cola Company 1997 Annual Report.
*Excludes products distributed by the Minute Maid Company.

Worldwide Beverage Consumption in 1997

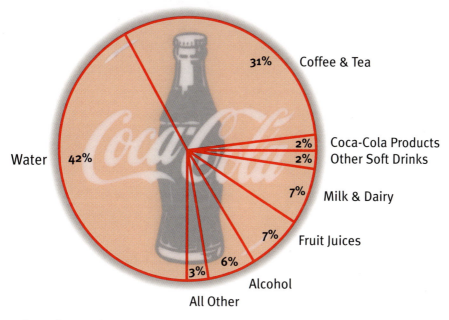

Source: The Coca-Cola Company 1997 Annual Report.

single day. To stay on top in the future, Coca-Cola must continue to grow, selling more Coke products in both the United States and in foreign countries. They must also come up with fresh ideas to keep consumers happy.

Selling new products to other countries can be a challenge. People from other countries may speak different languages and have different tastes than people in the United States. Companies like Coca-Cola must find out which products appeal to the residents of a particular country or they must create new products that they may like even better. In Japan, for example, Coca-Cola bottlers sell the Georgia Coffee® line along with Coke, while flavored teas are popular with Chinese consumers.

Reaching new Coke drinkers requires special advertising suited to each particular country, so Coca-Cola uses 25 different agencies to design advertisements for radio, television, newspapers, magazines, and billboards around the world.

As the Coca-Cola Company prepares its plans for the 21st century, the company intends to expand their network of bottlers and products into even more countries around the globe. It may be hard for Americans to believe, but there are still people in the world who have never had their first sip of Coke. The Coca-Cola Company plans to change that. Perhaps Coca-Cola will one day be the most popular drink in every country and truly become "the world's soft drink."

The Coca-Cola Foundation

Like many successful companies, the Coca-Cola Company wants to give something back to communities in the United States and other nations. In 1984, the company started The Coca-Cola Foundation to help fund education programs around the world. The foundation supports the Pipeline Program, aimed at keeping children from dropping out of school. It also funds global art and business-management education programs. The Coca-Cola Company offers a wide range of college scholarships through the foundation.

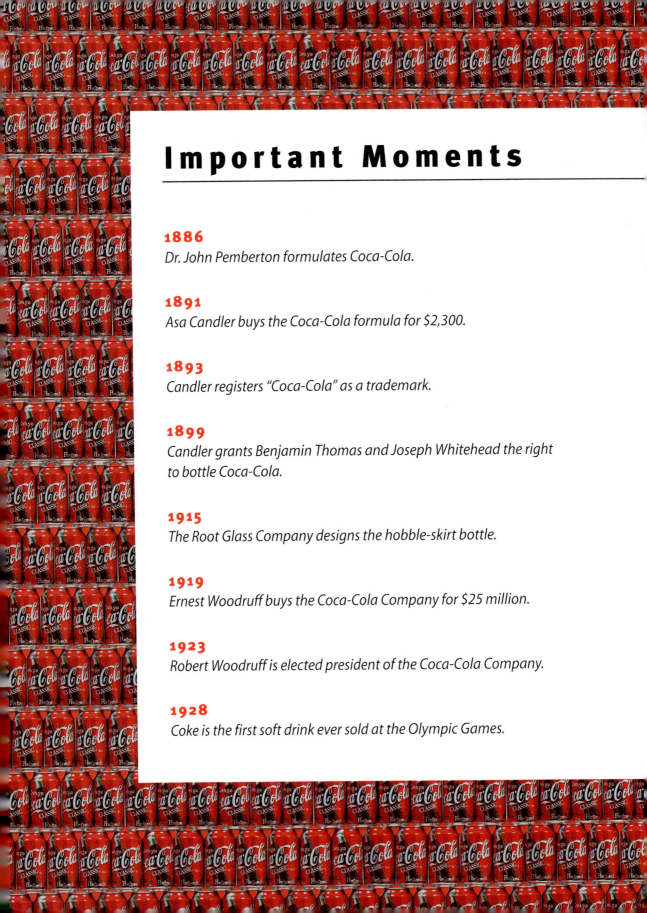

Important Moments

1886
Dr. John Pemberton formulates Coca-Cola.

1891
Asa Candler buys the Coca-Cola formula for $2,300.

1893
Candler registers "Coca-Cola" as a trademark.

1899
Candler grants Benjamin Thomas and Joseph Whitehead the right to bottle Coca-Cola.

1915
The Root Glass Company designs the hobble-skirt bottle.

1919
Ernest Woodruff buys the Coca-Cola Company for $25 million.

1923
Robert Woodruff is elected president of the Coca-Cola Company.

1928
Coke is the first soft drink ever sold at the Olympic Games.

1929
The Coca-Cola Company introduces its famous bell-shaped glasses.

1945
"Coke" becomes a registered trademark.

1960
The Coca-Cola Company adds its first new product line, called Fanta.

1985
The "cola wars" cause the Coca-Cola Company to change its formula and introduce New Coke. After Coke drinkers complain, the original formula is reintroduced with a new name, Coca-Cola Classic.

1987
The Coca-Cola Company introduces new juice drinks using the Minute Maid name.

1990
The World of Coca-Cola opens in Atlanta, Georgia.

1999
Drinkers of Diet Coke purchase an average of at least seven books per year. The company begins a marketing campaign to include excerpts from the works of popular authors with Diet Coke products.

Glossary

ad campaigns — Planned series of ads with a common theme.

carbonated — Relating to the use of carbon dioxide to make a soft drink bubbly.

consumers — People who buy and consume, or use, a product or service.

contracts — Written agreements made between two parties promising to meet certain obligations.

executives — A company's leaders, such as its president and top managers. Executives make important decisions for a company.

extracts — A concentrated substance that is extracted, or taken out of, its source, such as a plant or fruit. An extract has a stronger flavor or smell than its source.

independent bottlers — Businesspeople who pay to set up a bottling plant with their money but are given assistance from the soft-drink company. The Coca-Cola Company supplies independent bottlers with syrup to produce its products.

license — Permission granted to use a company name, slogan, or image.

market — To promote or advertise a product to consumers.

memorabilia — Objects that are reminders of the past.

pharmacist   A person who prepares and distributes medicines.

recycle   To process a used material (such as plastic, aluminum, or glass) so that it can be used again.

slogan   A short, attention-getting phrase used in advertising.

stimulants   Compounds, such as caffeine, that can make a person feel more awake or energetic. If people ingest too much of a stimulant, they can feel nervous or jittery.

technology   Science that is used to improve everyday life.

tonics   Mixtures designed to refresh and restore.

trademark   A symbol or name that belongs legally and exclusively to one company. It may also refer to something that is unique about a company.

Index

ad campaigns, 26-27
automatic fountain dispenser, 17, **18**

Biedenharn, Joseph, 11
bottling, 10-11, 19, 35

Candler, Asa, 7-9, 10, 16, 24, 37
cans, **16,** 19-20, **21, 29**
Coca-Cola
   bell-shaped glass, **14,** 15, 19, 27, 28
   and bottle design, 12, **13,** 15
   and carbonation, 5, 6
   and collectibles, 8, 9, 32-33
   commercials for, 25, 35, **36**
   and competition, 11-12, 26-30
   formula for, 5, 28-30
   name of, 5
   sales of, 6, 37, 39
   slogans for, 6, 7, 25, **26,** 31
   soldiers and, 17-18, **19, 20**
   syrup for, 5, 9, 10-11, 17
   trademarks for, 9
Coca-Cola Classic, 29-30
Coca-Cola Company, the
   and advertising, 5-6, 7-9, 24-25, **26,**
      31, 34-35, **36,** 40
   sale of, 7, 16
Coca-Cola Foundation, the, 41
Coca-Cola products, 23
   consumption of daily, 4, 9
   consumption of annually, 38
   international marketing of, 35, 40
   international sales of, 17-18, 38, 39-40
   introduction of, 20-22, 23
   marketing of, 7-9, 24-31, 39-41
Coke, see Coca-Cola
   and trademark name, 9

Coke Light, 22
cola wars, the, 26-30

Diet Coke, 22
Dyson, Brian, **30**

Eisenhower, Dwight, **28**
extracts, 5

Fanta, 20, 22

hobble-skirt bottle, 15

independent bottlers, 11, **12**

Jacob's Pharmacy, 5

license, 33

memorabilia, **8, 24,** 32-33, **34**
Minute Maid products, 22

New Coke, 29

Olympics, 17

Pemberton, John, 5-7, 12, 35, 37
Pepsi, 26-29
PET bottles, 19, 21

recycling, 20, **21**
Robinson, Frank, 5
Rockwell, Norman, 24
Root Glass Company, 15

Santa Claus, 33, **34**
slogans, 6, 7, 25, **26,** 31, 33

soda fountains, 5, **7,** 10, 17, 18, 19, 35
soldiers, 17-18, **19, 20**
Sprite, 22
stimulants, 22
Sundblom, Haddon, 33-34
Surge, 22

Tab, 22
Thomas, Benjamin, 11
tonics, 5, 7
trademark, 9

vending machines, 17

Whitehead, Joseph, 11
Woodruff, Ernest, 16
Woodruff, Robert Winship, 16-18
World of Coca-Cola, the, 33, 35, **35, 36**
World War I, **19**
World War II, 17-18, **20**

Items in bold print indicate illustration.

Further Information

BOOKS:

Applegate, Howard. *Coca-Cola: A History in Photographs 1930-1969.* Wisconsin: Voyageur Press, 1996.

Gould, William. *Coca-Cola.* Lincolnwood, IL: VGM Career Horizons, 1996.

Graham, Elizabeth Candler. *Cooking with Coca-Cola.* Nashville, TN: Hambleton Hill Publishers, 1994.

Zubrowski, Bernie. *Soda Science: Designing and Testing Soft Drinks.* NY: William Morrow & Co. Library, 1997.

WEB SITES:

Visit the Coca-Cola Company's official Web site:
http://www.cocacola.com

For more information about recycling:
http://www.envirosystemsinc.com

To visit the official Web site of the Coca-Cola Collectors:
http://www.geocities.com/Heartland/Meadows/7113

338.76
MAU

HOLMAN MIDDLE SCHOOL
LIBRARY
11055 ST. CHARLES ROCK ROAD
ST. ANN, MO 63074

DEMCO